OUR FAVORITE OLD HYMNS

**Some of the Old Ones We Love,
But We don't Get To Sing Them Anymore.**

Dedication

This is a book of selected hymns that have passed the test of many generations and continue to inspire families all over America and the world. These hymns are dedicated to the participants of our weekly Nursing Home Bible Studies. Even if they are suffering from Alzheimer's disease, they remember these songs and love to sing them again with us. They inspire us with their joy and exuberance when we play the recorded music. Now with this song book, many of them will be able to recall their church days, singing these same songs with a hymn book... We have found it amazing that with music, their old memories of these songs come back.

As John Milton Black wrote in his Hymn in 1893:

When the Roll is Called Up Yonder

When the trumpet of the Lord shall sound,
and time shall be no more,
And the morning breaks, eternal, bright and fair;
When the saved of earth shall gather over on the other shore,
And the roll is called up yonder,
I'll be there.

Blessings,

Ed & Gayle Griffiths

2017 Paperback Edition
Copyright 2017 Ed Griffiths
Shabbat Hollar Books and Games
All right reserved
ISBN-13:978-1546467991

Authorship for all songs is noted.
Cover photo is of the sun rising on the
eastern shore of the Sea of Galilee in Israel

Forward

Gayle and I were in Israel...

On that special morning, we were scheduled to take a trip on a fishing boat from Tiberius across the Sea of Galilee. The sun was just rising over the eastern shore, but the clouds were thick. We zipped up our jackets and boarded the fishing boat, on that misty overcast morning. The skies were dark, the wind was blowing and the seas were rough; choppy with whitecaps. It was not a great day to be out on the water. Our guides had told us that storms can come up very fast at any time; but we braved the weather and stood near the bow as the boat sailed out.

A young man with us was a worship leader at his church. Soon, he began to play and sing *"My God is an Awesome God"*.... So we all started singing with him as he played.

Then an amazing thing happened.
> The mist stopped.
> The seas calmed.
> The clouds started to break up.
> The sun peaked out at us.
> A flock of birds surrounded the boat.
> It became a beautiful day.
All the while we were singing that song.

We began to sing with more feeling as we understood that GOD had welcomed us, and HE was reminding us of how Jesus had calmed _that_ sea.

It's been twelve years since that day and we still have chills whenever we think of that morning and how we all felt the presence of GOD with us.

The picture on the cover was taken early that morning...
That song is included in this book.

Hymn Book Overview

This is a book of selected hymns that have passed the test of many generations and continue to inspire families all over America and the world.

We hope you enjoy singing them again….Ed & Gayle

Table of Contents

Amazing Grace

John Newton 1765

Amazing grace! How sweet the sound
That saved a wretch like me!
I once was lost, but now am found;
Was blind, but now I see.

'Twas grace that taught my heart to fear,
And grace my fears relieved;
How precious did that grace appear
The hour I first believed.

Through many dangers, toils and snares,
I have already come;
'Tis grace hath brought me safe thus far,
And grace will lead me home.

The Lord has promised good to me,
His word my hope secures;
He will my shield and portion be,
As long as life endures.

Yea, when this flesh and heart shall fail,
And mortal life shall cease,
I shall possess, within the veil,
A life of joy and peace.

The world shall soon dissolve like snow,
The sun refuse to shine;
But God, who called me here below,
Shall be forever mine.

When we've been there ten thousand years,
Bright shining as the sun,
We've no less days to sing God's praise
Than when we'd first begun.

Blessed Assurance

Phoebe Knapp 1873

Blessed assurance, Jesus is mine!
O what a foretaste of glory divine!
Heir of salvation, purchase of God,
Born of His Spirit, washed in His blood.

Refrain
This is my story, this is my song,
Praising my Savior, all the day long;
This is my story, this is my song,
Praising my Savior, all the day long.

Perfect submission, perfect delight,
Visions of rapture now burst on my sight;
Angels descending bring from above
Echoes of mercy, whispers of love.
Refrain

Perfect submission, all is at rest
I in my Savior am happy and blest,
Watching and waiting, looking above,
Filled with His goodness, lost in His love.
Refrain

Blessed be the Name

Charles Wesley 1739

Oh, for a thousand tongues to sing,
Blessed be the Name of the Lord!
The glories of my God and king!
Blessed be the Name of the Lord!

Refrain:
Blessed be the Name, blessed be the Name,
Blessed be the Name of the Lord!
Blessed be the Name, blessed be the Name,
Blessed be the Name of the Lord!

Jesus! the Name that charms our fears,
Blessed be the Name of the Lord!
''Tis music in the sinner's ears,
Blessed be the Name of the Lord!
Refrain

He breaks the pow'r of canceled sin,
Blessed be the Name of the Lord!
His blood can make the foulest clean,
Blessed be the Name of the Lord!
Refrain

I never shall forget that day,
Blessed be the Name of the Lord!
When Jesus washed my sins away,
Blessed be the Name of the Lord!
Refrain

Bringing in the Sheaves

Knowles Shaw 1874

Sowing in the morning, sowing seeds of kindness,
Sowing in the noontide and the dewy eve;
Waiting for the harvest, and the time of reaping,
We shall come rejoicing, bringing in the sheaves.

Refrain
Bringing in the sheaves, bringing in the sheaves,
We shall come rejoicing, bringing in the sheaves,
Bringing in the sheaves, bringing in the sheaves,
We shall come rejoicing, bringing in the sheaves,

Sowing in the sunshine, sowing in the shadows,
Fearing neither clouds nor winter's chilling breeze;
By and by the harvest, and the labor ended,
We shall come rejoicing, bringing in the sheaves.
Refrain

Going forth with weeping, sowing for the Master,
Though the loss sustained our spirit often grieves;
When our weeping's over, He will bid us welcome,
We shall come rejoicing, bringing in the sheaves.
Refrain

Count Your Blessings

Edmund O. Excell and Jonathan Oatman Jr. 1897

When upon life's billows you are tempest tossed,
When you are discouraged, thinking all is lost,
Count your many blessings, name them one by one,
And it will surprise you what the Lord hath done.

Refrain
Count your blessings, name them one by one,
Count your blessings, see what God hath done!
Count your blessings, name them one by one,
And it will surprise you what the Lord hath done.

Are you ever burdened with a load of care?
Does the cross seem heavy you are called to bear?
Count your many blessings, every doubt will fly,
And you will keep singing as the days go by.
Refrain

When you look at others with their lands and gold,
Think that Christ has promised you His wealth untold;
Count your many blessings. Wealth can never buy
Your reward in heaven, nor your home on high.
Refrain

So, amid the conflict whether great or small,
Do not be disheartened, God is over all;
Count your many blessings, angels will attend,
Help and comfort give you to your journey's end.
Refrain

Down by the Riverside

Slave Song prior to Civil War

<u>Gonna lay down my sword and shield:</u>
Down by the riverside
Down by the riverside
Down by the riverside

<u>Gonna lay down my sword and shield:</u>
Down by the riverside
Gonna study war no more.

Refrain:
I ain't gonna study war no more,
I ain't gonna study war no more,
Study war no more.
I ain't gonna study war no more,
I ain't gonna study war no more,
Study war no more.

<u>Do a verse for each of these lines followed by the *Refrain*</u>

Gonna stick my sword in the golden sand; etc.
Refrain

Gonna put on my long white robe; etc.
Refrain

Gonna put on my starry crown; etc.
Refrain

Gonna put on my golden shoes; etc.
Refrain

Gonna talk with the Prince of Peace; etc.
Refrain

Gonna shake hands around the world; etc.
Refrain

Go Tell it on the Mountain

John Wesley, Jr. 1907

Refrain
Go, tell it on the mountain,
Over the hills and everywhere
Go, tell it on the mountain,
That Jesus Christ is born.

While shepherds kept their watching
Over silent flocks by night
Behold throughout the heavens
There shone a holy light.
Refrain

The shepherds feared and trembled,
When lo! above the earth,
Rang out the angels chorus
That hailed the Savior's birth.
Refrain

Down in a lowly manger
The humble Christ was born
And God sent us salvation
That blessed Christmas morn.
Refrain

He Lives

Alfred Henry Ackley 1933

I serve a risen Saviour, He's in the world today
I know that He is living, whatever men may say
I see His hand of mercy, I hear His voice of cheer
And just the time I need Him He's always near

Refrain:
He lives (He lives), He lives (He lives), Christ Jesus lives
today
He walks with me and talks with me
Along life's narrow way
He lives (He lives), He lives (He lives), Salvation to impart
You ask me how I know He lives?
He lives within my heart

In all the world around me I see His loving care
And though my heart grows weary I never will despair
I know that He is leading, through all the stormy blast
The day of His appearing will come at last
Refrain

Rejoice, rejoice, O Christian Lift up your voice and sing
Eternal hallelujahs to Jesus Christ, the King
The Hope of all who seek Him, the Help of all who find
None other is so loving, so good and kind
Refrain

His Name is Wonderful

Audrey Mieir 1959

His Name is Wonderful
His Name is Wonderful
His Name is Wonderful
Jesus My Lord

He is the Mighty King
Master of everything
His Name is Wonderful
Jesus My Lord

He's the Great shepherd
The Rock of All Ages
Almighty God is He

Bow down before Him
Love and adore Him
His Name is Wonderful
Jesus My Lord

Holy, Holy, Holy! Lord God Almighty

Reginald Heber 1826

Holy, holy, holy! Lord God Almighty!
Early in the morning our song shall rise to Thee;
Holy, holy, holy, merciful and mighty!
God in three Persons, blessed Trinity!

Holy, holy, holy! All the saints adore Thee,
Casting down their golden crowns around the glassy sea;
Cherubim and seraphim falling down before Thee,
Who was, and is, and evermore shall be.

Holy, holy, holy! though the darkness hide Thee,
Though the eye of sinful man Thy glory may not see;
Only Thou art holy; there is none beside Thee,
Perfect in power, in love, and purity.

Holy, holy, holy! Lord God Almighty!
All Thy works shall praise Thy Name, in earth, and sky,
and sea;
Holy, holy, holy; merciful and mighty!
God in three Persons, blessed Trinity!

How Great Thou Art

Stuart K. Hine 1885

O Lord my God, when I in awesome wonder,
Consider all the worlds Thy hands have made;
I see the stars, I hear the rolling thunder,
Thy power throughout the universe displayed.

Refrain:
Then sings my soul, my Savior God, to Thee,
How great Thou art! How great Thou art!
Then sings my soul, My Savior God, to Thee,
How great Thou art! How great Thou art!

When through the woods, and forest glades I wander,
And hear the birds sing sweetly in the trees.
When I look down, from lofty mountain grandeur
And hear the brook, and feel the gentle breeze.
Refrain

And when I think, that God, His Son not sparing;
Sent Him to die, I scarce can take it in;
That on the cross, my burden gladly bearing,
He bled and died to take away my sin.
Refrain

When Christ shall come, with shout of acclamation,
And take me home, what joy shall fill my heart.
Then I shall bow, in humble adoration,
And then proclaim, "My God, how great Thou art!"
Refrain

I'll Fly Away

Albert E. Brumley 1929

Some bright morning when this life is over
I'll fly away
To that home on God's celestial shore
I'll fly away

Refrain:
I'll fly away, oh glory
I'll fly away in the morning
When I die, Hallelujah by and by
I'll fly away

When the shadows of this life have gone
I'll fly away
Like a bird from these prison walls I'll fly
I'll fly away

Refrain

Oh, how glad and happy when we meet
I'll fly away
No more cold iron shackles on my feet
I'll fly away

Refrain

Refrain

In the Garden

C. Austin Miles 1912

I come to the garden alone
While the dew is still on the roses
And the voice I hear falling on my ear
The Son of God discloses.

Refrain
And He walks with me, and He talks with me,
And He tells me I am His own;
And the joy we share as we tarry there,
None other has ever known.

He speaks, and the sound of His voice,
Is so sweet the birds hush their singing,
And the melody that He gave to me
Within my heart is ringing.
Refrain

I'd stay in the garden with Him
Though the night around me be falling,
But He bids me go; through the voice of woe
His voice to me is calling.
Refrain

It is Well With My Soul

Philip Paul Bliss and Horatio Spafford 1873
When peace, like a river, attendeth my way,
When sorrows like sea billows roll;
Whatever my lot, Thou has taught me to say,
It is well, it is well, with my soul.

Refrain
It is well, with my soul,
It is well, with my soul,
It is well, it is well, with my soul.

Though Satan should buffet, though trials should come,
Let this blest assurance control,
That Christ has regarded my helpless estate,
And hath shed His own blood for my soul.
Refrain

My sin, oh, the bliss of this glorious thought!
My sin, not in part but the whole,
Is nailed to the cross, and I bear it no more,
Praise the Lord, praise the Lord, O my soul!
Refrain

For me, be it Christ, be it Christ hence to live:
If Jordan above me shall roll,
No pang shall be mine, for in death as in life
Thou wilt whisper Thy peace to my soul.
Refrain

But, Lord, 'tis for Thee, for Thy coming we wait,
The sky, not the grave, is our goal;
Oh trump of the angel! Oh voice of the Lord!
Blessed hope, blessed rest of my soul!
Refrain

And Lord, haste the day when my faith shall be sight,
The clouds be rolled back as a scroll;
The trump shall resound, and the Lord shall descend,
Even so, it is well with my soul.
Refrain

Jesus Loves Me

William Batchelder Bradbury 1860

Jesus loves me! This I know,
For the Bible tells me so.
Little ones to Him belong;
They are weak, but He is strong.

Refrain:
Yes, Jesus loves me!
Yes, Jesus loves me!
Yes, Jesus loves me!
The Bible tells me so.

Jesus loves me! This I know,
As He loved so long ago,
Taking children on His knee,
Saying, "Let them come to Me."
Refrain

Jesus loves me still today,
Walking with me on my way,
Wanting as a friend to give
Light and love to all who live.
Refrain

Jesus loves me! He who died
Heaven's gate to open wide;
He will wash away my sin,
Let His little child come in.
Refrain

Jesus loves me! He will stay
Close beside me all the way;
Thou hast bled and died for me,
I will henceforth live for Thee.
Refrain

Jesus Paid It All

Elvina M. Hall 1865

I hear the Savior say,
"Thy strength indeed is small;
Child of weakness, watch and pray,
Find in Me thine all in all."

Refrain:
Jesus paid it all,
All to Him I owe;
Sin had left a crimson stain,
He washed it white as snow.

For nothing good have I
Whereby Thy grace to claim,
I'll wash my garments white
In the blood of Calv'ry's Lamb.
Refrain

And now complete in Him
My robe His righteousness,
Close sheltered 'neath His side,
I am divinely blest.
Refrain

Lord, now indeed I find
Thy power and Thine alone,
Can change the leper's spots
And melt the heart of stone.
Refrain

When from my dying bed
My ransomed soul shall rise,
"Jesus died my soul to save,"
Shall rend the vaulted skies.
Refrain

And when before the throne
I stand in Him complete,
I'll lay my trophies down
All down at Jesus' feet.   *Refrain*

Just a Closer Walk

Unknown, Traditional Gospel Song

I am weak, but Thou art strong;
Jesus, keep me from all wrong;
I'll be satisfied as long
As I walk, let me walk close to Thee.

Refrain:
Just a closer walk with Thee,
Grant it, Jesus, is my plea,
Daily walking close to Thee,
Let it be, dear Lord, let it be.

Through this world of toil and snares,
If I falter, Lord, who cares?
Who with me my burden shares?
None but Thee, dear Lord, none but Thee.
Refrain

When my feeble life is o'er,
Time for me will be no more;
Guide me gently, safely o'er
To Thy kingdom shore, to Thy shore.
Refrain

Love Lifted Me

James Rowe and Howard E. Smith 1912

I was sinking deep in sin, far from the peaceful shore,
Very deeply stained within, sinking to rise no more,
But the Master of the sea, heard my despairing cry,
From the waters lifted me, now safe am I.

Refrain:
Love lifted me! Love lifted me!
When nothing else could help
Love lifted me!

All my heart to Him I give, ever to Him I'll cling
In His blessed presence live, ever His praises sing,
Love so mighty and so true, merits my soul's best songs,
Faithful, loving service too, to Him belongs
Refrain

Souls in danger look above, Jesus completely saves,
He will lift you by His love, out of the angry waves.
He's the Master of the sea, billows His will obey,
He your Savior wants to be, be saved today.
Refrain

Nearer my God to Thee

Sarah Adams and Lowell Mason 1841

Nearer, my God, to Thee, nearer to Thee!
E'en though it be a cross that raiseth me,
Still all my song shall be, nearer, my God, to Thee.

Refrain:
Nearer, my God, to Thee,
Nearer to Thee!

Though like the wanderer, the sun gone down,
Darkness be over me, my rest a stone.
Yet in my dreams I'd be nearer, my God to Thee.
Refrain

There let the way appear, steps unto Heav'n;
All that Thou sendest me, in mercy given;
Angels to beckon me nearer, my God, to Thee.
Refrain

Then, with my waking thoughts bright with Thy praise,
Out of my stony griefs Bethel I'll raise;
So by my woes to be nearer, my God, to Thee.
Refrain

Or, if on joyful wing cleaving the sky,
Sun, moon, and stars forgot, upward I'll fly,
Still all my song shall be, nearer, my God, to Thee.
Refrain

There in my Father's home, safe and at rest,
There in my Savior's love, perfectly blest;
Age after age to be, nearer my God to Thee.
Refrain

Old Time Religion

Charles D. Tillman - Traditional Gospel Song 1889

Refrain:
Give me that old time religion
Give me that old time religion,
'Give me that old time religion,
And it's good enough for me.

It was good for our mothers.
It was good for our mothers.
It was good for our mothers.
And it's good enough for me.
Refrain

Makes me love everybody.
Makes me love everybody.
Makes me love everybody.
And it's good enough for me.
Refrain

It has saved our fathers.
It has saved our fathers.
It has saved our fathers.
And it's good enough for me.
Refrain

It will do when I am dying.
It will do when I am dying.
It will do when I am dying.
And it's good enough for me.
Refrain

It will take us all to heaven.
It will take us all to heaven.
It will take us all to heaven.
And it's good enough for me.
Refrain

Old Rugged Cross

George Bennard 1912

On a hill far away stood an old rugged cross,
The emblem of suffering and shame;
And I love that old cross where the dearest and best
For a world of lost sinners was slain.

Refrain:
So I'll cherish the old rugged cross,
Till my trophies at last I lay down;
I will cling to the old rugged cross,
And exchange it some day for a crown.

O that old rugged cross, so despised by the world,
Has a wondrous attraction for me;
For the dear Lamb of God left His glory above
To bear it to dark Calvary.
Refrain

In that old rugged cross, stained with blood so divine,
A wondrous beauty I see,
For 'twas on that old cross Jesus suffered and died,
To pardon and sanctify me.
Refrain

To the old rugged cross I will ever be true;
Its shame and reproach gladly bear;
Then He'll call me some day to my home far away,
Where His glory forever I'll share.
Refrain

Our God is an Awesome God

Rich Mullins 1988

Refrain
Our God is an awesome God
He reigns from Heaven above
With wisdom, power and love
Our God is an awesome God
Refrain

When He rolls up His sleeves
He ain't just putting on the ritz
(Our God is an awesome God)
There is thunder in His footsteps
And lightning in His fists
(Our God is an awesome God)
Refrain

The Lord wasn't joking when
He kicked them out of Eden
It wasn't for no reason that He shed His blood
Coming soon, you better be believing
(Our God is an awesome God)
Refrain

When the sky was starless in the void of the night
(Our God is an awesome God)
He spoke into the darkness and created the light
(Our God is an awesome God)
Refrain

Judgment and wrath He poured out on Sodom
Mercy and grace, He gave us at the cross
Hope that you have not too quickly forgotten that
(Our God is an awesome God)

Our God is an awesome God
Our God is an awesome God

Rock of Ages

Augustus Montague Toplady and Thomas Hastings 1763

Rock of Ages, cleft for me,
Let me hide myself in Thee;
Let the water and the blood,
From Thy wounded side which flowed,
Be of sin the double cure;
Save from wrath and make me pure.

Not the labor of my hands
Can fulfill Thy law's demands;
Could my zeal no respite know,
Could my tears forever flow,
All for sin could not atone;
Thou must save, and Thou alone.

Nothing in my hand I bring,
Simply to the cross I cling;
Naked, come to Thee for dress;
Helpless look to Thee for grace;
Foul, I to the fountain fly;
Wash me, Savior, or I die.

While I draw this fleeting breath,
When mine eyes shall close in death,
When I soar to worlds unknown,
See Thee on Thy judgment throne,
Rock of Ages, cleft for me,
Let me hide myself in Thee

Satisfied

Unknown

Well satisfied with Jesus, satisfied with Jesus
Said He would be my comfort
Said He would be my guide
Well, well I looked at my hands, my hands looked new
I looked at my feet and they did too
Ever since that wonderful day
My soul's been satisfied

Refrain:
Well, satisfied with Jesus, satisfied with Jesus
Because said He would be my comfort
Said He would be my guide
Well, well I looked at my hands, my hands looked new
I looked at my feet and they did too
Ever since that wonderful day
My soul's been satisfied

The Lord moves in mysterious ways
His wonders to perform
He plants His feet on every step
And then He rides on every storm
Well He fixed my feet for runnin', boys
Then my eyes were opened up wide
He fixed my tongue so I could say
"Praise God, I'm satisfied."
Refrain

Well it was way down yonder in the valley, boys
I was wandering' all alone
And it was there I met my Jesus,
You know He claimed me for His own
And then He put His arms all around me there
And then He drew me up to His side
Refrain

Shall We Gather at the River

Robert Lowry 1864

Shall we gather at the river,
Where bright angel feet have trod,
With its crystal tide forever
Flowing by the throne of God?

Refrain:
Yes, we'll gather at the river,
The beautiful, the beautiful river;
Gather with the saints at the river
That flows by the throne of God.

On the margin of the river,
Washing up its silver spray,
We will talk and worship ever,
All the happy golden day.
Refrain

Ere we reach the shining river,
Lay we every burden down;
Grace our spirits will deliver,
And provide a robe and crown.
Refrain

At the smiling of the river,
Mirror of the Savior's face,
Saints, whom death will never sever,
Lift their songs of saving grace.
Refrain

Soon we'll reach the silver river,
Soon our pilgrimage will cease;
Soon our happy hearts will quiver
With the melody of peace.
Refrain

Since Jesus Came into My Heart

Rufus H. McDaniel 1914

What a wonderful change in my life has been wrought
Since Jesus came into my heart;
I have light in my soul for which long I have sought,
Since Jesus came into my heart.

Refrain:
Since Jesus came into my heart,
Since Jesus came into my heart;
Floods of joy o'er my soul like the sea billows roll,
Since Jesus came into my heart.

I have ceased from my wand'ring and going astray,
Since Jesus came into my heart;
And my sins which were many are all washed away,
Since Jesus came into my heart.
I'm possessed of a hope that is steadfast and sure,
Since Jesus came into my heart;
And no dark clouds of doubt now my pathway
obscure,
Since Jesus came into my heart.

There's a light in the valley of death now for me,
Since Jesus came into my heart;
And the gates of the City beyond I can see,
Since Jesus came into my heart.
I shall go there to dwell in that City I know,
Since Jesus came into my heart;
And I'm happy, so happy as onward I go,
Since Jesus came into my heart.

Stand up for Jesus

George Duffield, Jr. 1858

Stand up, stand up for Jesus, ye soldiers of the cross;
Lift high His royal banner, it must not suffer loss.
From victory unto victory His army shall He lead,
Till every foe is vanquished, and Christ is Lord indeed.

Stand up, stand up for Jesus, the solemn watchword
hear;
If while ye sleep He suffers, away with shame and fear;
Where'er ye meet with evil, within you or without,
Charge for the God of battles, and put the foe to rout.

Stand up, stand up for Jesus, the trumpet call obey;
Forth to the mighty conflict, in this His glorious day.
Ye that are brave now serve Him against unnumbered
foes;
Let courage rise with danger, and strength to strength
oppose.

Stand up, stand up for Jesus, stand in His strength alone;
The arm of flesh will fail you, ye dare not trust your own.
Put on the Gospel armor, each piece put on with prayer;
Where duty calls or danger, be never wanting there.

Stand up, stand up for Jesus, each soldier to his post,
Close up the broken column, and shout through all the
host:
Make good the loss so heavy, in those that still remain,
And prove to all around you that death itself is gain.

Stand up, stand up for Jesus, the strife will not be long;
This day the noise of battle, the next the victor's song.
To those who vanquish evil a crown of life shall be;
They with the King of Glory shall reign eternally.

Sweet By and By

Joseph Philbrick Webster 1868

There's a land that is fairer than day,
And by faith we can see it afar;
For the Father waits over the way
To prepare us a dwelling place there.

Refrain:
In the sweet in the sweet
By and by, by and by,
We shall meet on that beautiful shore;
In the sweet in the sweet
By and by by and by
We shall meet on that beautiful shore.

We shall sing on that beautiful shore
The melodious songs of the blest,
And our spirits shall sorrow no more
Not a sigh for the blessing of rest.
Refrain:

To our bountiful father above
We will offer our tribute of praise;
For the glorious gift of His love
And the blessings that hallow our days.
Refrain:

There is Power in the Blood

Lewis E. Jones 1899

Would you be free from the burden of sin?
There's power in the blood, power in the blood;
Would you o'er evil a victory win?
There's wonderful power in the blood.

Refrain:
There is power, power, wonder working power
In the blood of the Lamb;
There is power, power, wonder working power
In the precious blood of the Lamb.

Would you be free from your passion and pride?
There's power in the blood, power in the blood;
Come for a cleansing to Calvary's tide;
There's wonderful power in the blood.
Refrain

Would you be whiter, much whiter than snow?
There's power in the blood, power in the blood;
Sin stains are lost in its life giving flow.
There's wonderful power in the blood.
Refrain

Would you do service for Jesus your King?
There's power in the blood, power in the blood;
Would you live daily His praises to sing?
There's wonderful power in the blood.
Refrain

Tis So Sweet to Trust in Jesus

Louisa M.R.Stead and Willian J. Kirkpatrick 1882

Tis so sweet to trust in Jesus,
And to take Him at His Word;
Just to rest upon His promise,
And to know, "Thus says the Lord!"

Refrain:
Jesus, Jesus, how I trust Him!
How I've proved Him o'er and o'er
Jesus, Jesus, precious Jesus!
O for grace to trust Him more!

O how sweet to trust in Jesus,
Just to trust His cleansing blood;
And in simple faith to plunge me
'Neath the healing, cleansing flood!
Refrain

Yes, 'tis sweet to trust in Jesus,
Just from sin and self to cease;
Just from Jesus simply taking
Life and rest, and joy and peace.
Refrain

I'm so glad I learned to trust Thee,
Precious Jesus, Savior, Friend;
And I know that Thou art with me,
Wilt be with me to the end.
Refrain

What a Friend We Have in Jesus

Joseph M. Scriven and Charles C. Converse 1855

What a friend we have in Jesus,
all our sins and griefs to bear!
What a privilege to carry
everything to God in prayer!
O what peace we often forfeit,
O what needless pain we bear,
all because we do not carry
everything to God in prayer.

Have we trials and temptations?
Is there trouble anywhere?
We should never be discouraged;
take it to the Lord in prayer.
Can we find a friend so faithful
who will all our sorrows share?
Jesus knows our every weakness;
take it to the Lord in prayer.

Are we weak and heavy laden,
cumbered with a load of care?
Precious Savior, still our refuge;
take it to the Lord in prayer.
Do thy friends despise, forsake thee?
Take it to the Lord in prayer!
In his arms he'll take and shield thee;
thou wilt find a solace there.

When the Roll Is Called Up Yonder

John Milton Black 1893

When the trumpet of the Lord shall sound, and time shall
be no more,
And the morning breaks, eternal, bright and fair;
When the saved of earth shall gather over on the other
shore,
And the roll is called up yonder, I'll be there.

Refrain:
When the roll, is called up yon-der,
When the roll, is called up yon-der,
When the roll, is called up yon-der,
When the roll is called up yonder I'll be there.

On that bright and cloudless morning when the dead in
Christ shall rise,
And the glory of His resurrection share;
When His chosen ones shall gather to their home beyond
the skies,
And the roll is called up yonder, I'll be there.
Refrain

Let us labor for the Master from the dawn till setting sun,
Let us talk of all His wondrous love and care;
Then when all of life is over, and our work on earth is
done,
And the roll is called up yonder, I'll be there.
Refrain

When They Ring those Golden Bells

Dion De Marbelle 1887

There's a land beyond the river,
That we call the sweet forever,
And we only reach that shore by faith's decree;
One by one we'll gain the portals,
There to dwell with the immortals,
When they ring those golden bells for you and me.

Refrain:
Don't you hear the bells now ringing?
Don't you hear the angels singing?
'Tis the glory hallelujah Jubilee.
In that far off sweet forever,
Just beyond the shining river,
When they ring those golden bells for you and me.

We shall know no sin or sorrow,
In that haven of tomorrow,
When our barque shall sail beyond the silver sea;
We shall only know the blessing
Of our Father's sweet caressing,
When they ring those golden bells for you and me.
Refrain

When our days shall know their number,
And in death we sweetly slumber,
When the King commands the spirit to be free;
Nevermore with anguish laden,
We shall reach that lovely Eden,
When they ring those golden bells for you and me.
Refrain

Appendix

Sources of Hymn Lyrics

These are internet sites with thousands of free lyrics
https://www.songandpraise.org/
https://hymnlyrics.org/
http://www.elyrics.net/

Sources of the Recorded Music

Recorded music for all Hymns is available on ITunes.

Other Books in this Collection

Available on Amazon.com

Companion Guides (use your favorite bible for book's scripture)

The Book of Revelation
- A Study guide of Revelation with references to Old and New Testament scripture. (Available)

The Book of Isaiah (In Process – expected September 2017)
- A Study guide of Isaiah with references to Old and New Testament scripture.

The Book of Daniel (to be scheduled)
- A Study guide of Isaiah with references to Old and New Testament scripture.

Other Works Available

Works of the Messiah (all scripture included)
- A Study Guide of Jesus' Ministry, using Psalms, Miracles and Parables. (Available)

Reflections on Psalms (all scripture included)
- A personal testimony written by Gayle Griffiths and keyed to events in Psalms (Available)

Other Works Scheduled

Heroes of Faith (In Process –expected June 2017)
- A study of the lives people of Bible, as denoted in The Book of Hebrews chapter 11 showing their faith in GOD.

Favorite Bible events with Commentary (expected late 2017)
1) The Ministry of John the Baptist
2) Noah and the Ark
3) TBD

Printed in Great Britain
by Amazon